The Splendid Little Book
All Things Cat

by Bob Lovka

illustrations by Setsu Broderick

BOWTIE
P R E S S

To Larry Sloan, whose splendid little books
are always the "cat's meow."
-B.L.
To Kyle, Raulie, Genna, and Parker.
-S.B.

Ruth Berman, editor-in-chief
Nick Clemente, special consultant
Cathe Jacobi, designer

Library of Congress Cataloging-in-Publication Data

Lovka, Bob, Date.
   The splendid little book of all things cat / Bob Lovka ;
  illustrations by Setsu Broderick.
    p.   cm.
  ISBN 1-889540-28-5
  1. Cats—Miscellanea. 2. Cats—Health—Miscellanea. I. Title.
  SF447.L66 1998
  636.8—dc21   97-32165
                                       CIP

BowTie™ Press
3 Burroughs
Irvine, California 92618

Manufactured in the United States of America
First Printing April 1998
10 9 8 7 6 5 4 3 2

CONTENTS

A Note from Bob   4

1. The Wonderful World of Cats   5

2. Food for Thought   22

3. Is There a Cat Doctor in the House?   31

4. Home Sweet Home   47

5. Let's Get Physical!   62

6. The Kitten Korner   74

7. The Not-so-Great Outdoors   85

8. Special Considerations   96

A Note from Bob

Welcome to the splendid world of cats! Whether you are owned by a cat or just on friendly terms, this lively little book answers some questions, surprises you with some fun facts, and teaches you a few things about caring for and cuddling up to your feline friend.

From the first day a cat adopts you, life takes on a different glow. No matter if your cat is an independent diva, a curious companion, or a mischievous little rascal, your life will be changed. Cats keep their own schedules, and never (well, hardly ever) are predictable, choosing to see the world in their own magical ways. The information contained here can give you some insight into the world a cat sees; and by taking to heart the tips and advice you find along the way, you enhance the health, happiness, and well-being of your furry friend. A cat wouldn't have it any other way!

The Wonderful World of Cats

They're fun, they're friends,
they're family members,
but did you know…?
Welcome to the wonderful world of cats!

Does your cat rub her face against you? This is an affectionate way for your cat to mark you with scent from her cheek glands. Face it, you are owned and you are territory!

If your cat curls her tail up, arches her back, and walks sideways toward another cat, she is not doing a John Wayne impression but is signaling that she wants to play. The second cat adopts a similar pose if the invitation is accepted.

chapter 1

Is it playing or is it fighting? Sometimes it's difficult to tell the difference, but one clue is that play is measurably quieter and does not result in injury. And, after play, neither cat seems afraid of the other.

Cats are nocturnal by nature. However, If your cat's nighttime habits and tiptoe wanderings disturb your sleep, give her a quarter teaspoon of chamomile tea. (You might try a cup yourself before turning in!)

It is helpful to understand the social order of each cat in a multicat household. A subordinate cat often offers to groom a dominant one. Then they switch roles with the groomer becoming the groomed.

Does a black cat crossing your path always mean bad luck? Not everywhere! A French superstition holds that finding a single white hair in a black cat's coat brings wealth or true love. And the Japanese believe that certain ills are cured by black cats!

Not all white cats are albinos. A true albino cat has no eye color. Her eyes appear red due to the blood vessels at the back of the eyes.

Did you know that the varying color you see on a Siamese cat is determined by the cat's body temperature? The cooler parts of the cat—those away from the heart—are darker; the warmer areas are lighter. Siamese kittens are born without these color points because they are exposed to a uniform temperature in the womb.

chapter 1

A white cat with color only on her head and tail is called a van. If a van has one to three small spots of body color, she is classified as a harlequin.

Tabbies traditionally have facial markings that conform to the letter M. The body stripes on a mackerel tabby look like fish bones. A classic tabby has a symmetrical pattern of curved stripes on each side.

A shorthaired cat grows an average of sixty feet of hair a day—luckily, not all on one strand! See why cats shed so much?

Kitty Alert! Cats and chocolate don't mix. A portion of chocolate can be toxic to your feline friend. For cats, it's better mouse than mousse!

chapter 1

The aptly coined term "cat fancy" means the breeding and showing of cats. The first cat show was held in 1875 in London; the first American cat show came twenty years later. *Cat Fancy* magazine made its debut in 1965; and a famously fancy cat named Sylvester came on the scene in 1945.

Strictly speaking, a calico cat is white with solid patches of red and black. A tortoiseshell has a tweed-type coat with black hairs mixed with red hairs. A tortie-and-white is a tortoiseshell that also has some white. All three types are usually female.

They're called catnaps for a reason! Your average cat dozes eighteen to nineteen hours a day, although not in one long stretch. The stretching comes later.

Ever notice how a cat gravitates to the one person in the room who doesn't love cats? Animal behaviorists believe that cats feel less threatened by someone who ignores them.

Spay means to sterilize a female cat. This procedure, even if done before the first heat or pregnancy, has no adverse long-term effects on her behavior. Generally, the female no longer roams to find a mate. Spay/USA is a national low-cost spay and neuter referral service. Call (800) 248-SPAY for information.

Spay or neuter your pet before sexual behaviors begin to develop and before females have their first heat. This means a female should be spayed by six months of age and males neutered between seven and nine months.

Chapter 1

An "apron of skin" hanging below the abdomen is one sign of an overweight cat. Another is having an apron that won't go around the cat at all! Keep your cat healthy and happy—not too fat nor too thin. A healthy cat's ribs can easily be felt when you run your fingers along her sides. No love handles allowed!

I want attention! Cats with submissive personalities might at times display "sympathy behaviors"—actions designed to attract attention. For example, a limp that appears on one side and then on the other is likely a sympathy lameness. The best prescription is extra love!

Sniffling, Sneezing, Gasping Allergies

How frustrating to be a cat lover allergic to cats! Allergies get in the way of the best of bondings. The allergic reaction is not caused by the cat hair itself; the problematic allergen is a protein found in the saliva and skin of cats. This protein attaches to hair when the cat grooms, so cat hair is guilty by association. Small comfort—runny noses and itchy eyes can't tell the difference. Yet, 30 percent of cat owners are allergic to their pets and choose to live with the problems. Taking some precautions can help you coexist with fewer symptoms:

🐾 Keep your cat out of the bedroom. This allows for an overnight respite and an uncontaminated "safe house" from the worst exposure to allergens.

🐾 Fleas and worms cause cats to scratch and lick, the two activities that introduce allergenic saliva and dander to the air. Keeping the cat free of parasites can lessen your reaction.

❀ Have someone else maintain a strict schedule of grooming the cat, ideally in a separate room.

❀ Most allergic cat owners need all the relief they can get. Room-capacity air cleaners can remove nearly all the airborne cat allergens if the cleaners are equipped with high-efficiency particulate air (HEPA) filters.

❀ Allergic owners feel they should vacuum frequently. Unfortunately, this stirs up tiny allergen particles, which causes even more suffering. Damp mopping raises less dust than vacuuming and is worth a try, especially in the bedroom. If you must use a traditional vacuum cleaner, enlist help. You have a valid reason to tell someone else to vacuum while you go have fun!

❀ The allergy-sufferer feels better in an environment furnished with leather, glass, chrome, and plastic. Although this could be like living inside a 1966 Chevrolet Impala, it holds less dander and allergens than woven fabric. Wood flooring is also a big help.

❀ Over-the-counter antihistamines and prescription allergy blockers can offer some relief. Allergy shots are expensive but effective, especially when used in conjunction with other precautions.

❀ Alas, there is no cure-all to cat allergies. And sufferers are usually allergic to many other substances as well. If you can remove other sources of allergens from your surroundings, it might be easier to live with your cat—someone you don't want to remove at all!

Cats have no innate sense of right or wrong behavior. They're instinctual and behave the way nature dictates. If odd behavior arises, determine what the behavior is in response to—illness, fear, insecurity—and treat the cause.

Crime and Punishment? Punishment for bad behavior only destroys a cat's trust in you and is confusing. To be effectual, any correcting of a cat's behavior must be done as you literally catch Kitty in the act. Clap your hands or command "No!" in a strong voice.

chapter 1

Is Kitty reluctant to drink from the water bowl? Raise the bowl to chin or throat level. Some cats fear dunking their noses when the water surface is at ground level.

Cats use their sense of smell as a means of identification. The best way to introduce yourself to a cat? Let her sniff your hair!

A cat who wants to play with another cat often stands over that cat with her mouth open. A cooperative playmate lies on her back with all four legs extended. The longer the cats know each other, the more attuned they'll be to each other's play signals. Felines are quite adept at body language!

Cats like to stay neat and clean. If your cat or kitten shows little interest in grooming herself, have her examined by a veterinarian. Internal parasites could be the cause.

To encourage good litter box habits, consider using a fine-grained litter. Cats seem to prefer a mixture that is akin to the texture of sand.

Although tomcats spray most often, altered males and females can spray, too. Sometimes you just can't win. A cat marks his territory as a warning to other cats and as reassurance to himself that the sprayed area is his possession.

Place the litter box in a quiet location away from family traffic. Hustle and bustle is not the way to... go.

The most popular filler for cat litter is clay. You can also find wheat- or cedar-based fillers. Active enzymes in the wheat eliminate odors. Cedar has a natural scent that repels fleas. Both are flushable.

Food For Thought

Whether she's a finicky gourmet or he's a
fast-food freak, there's a lot to learn
about feeding a cat!

Never biting the hand that feeds… Studies show that a pet is more likely to eat when offered something from her owner's hand, regardless of what food is offered. Try the personal touch with a finicky eater!

Kitty Alert! Don't feed your cat raw eggs; they are a potential source of salmonella poisoning. Any food you would cook for your own use should be cooked for Kitty, too.

In general, cats show a marked intolerance to milk. Cats allergic to milk and milk products can suffer diarrhea and vomiting. Calcium is important for your cat and is available in a nutritionally balanced cat food. For everyday drinking, H_2O is the way to go.

Indoor cats have a tendency to gain weight rather easily since they don't have as much opportunity to exercise as outdoor cats. If your cat is putting on the poundage, check with your vet about the advisability of feeding a reduced-fat cat food or one formulated for less-active cats.

Tuna by the tablespoon! If your cat loves canned tuna for humans, restrict it to treat status—an occasional tablespoon or two. Too much can create a vitamin E deficiency in cats.

chapter 2

Cats like to munch on fresh greens occasionally. Give your indoor cats a treat by growing pots of grass and catnip for them.

A kitten's nutritional needs are much different from those of an adult cat. Feed a kitten a balanced diet of canned or dry food that is specifically labeled as being formulated for kittens.

Breakfast, lunch, and dinner? Not necessary. Cat feedings should be twice a day. A cat's normal saliva needs time to cleanse the mouth between feedings. Constant food access increases nibbling which means more plaque and tartar development, not to mention excess weight.

Food for Thought

Looking at Labels

Know what you're paying for. Pet food labels list ingredients in descending order of content. If water and ground mouse whiskers top the list, you are not getting "salmon fillet."

Words in a product name must conform to regulations. By law, a "turkey cat food" label must contain at least 95 percent turkey by weight. A modified title, however, such as "turkey dinner," can contain as little as 25 percent turkey.

INGREDIENTS: Ground mouse whiskers, Water....

When it comes to cat food ingredients, wheat, ground corn, corn gluten, and rice are good plant sources of carbohydrates and some protein. Their presence will be listed on the label.

Complete and balanced cat foods are labeled as such. This is a quality standard that meets a cat's nutritional needs. Foods not meeting this standard are labeled as "intended for intermittent or supplemental feeding only."

Minerals are important in your cat's diet. The Big Four are calcium, phosphorous, sodium, and potassium. Magnesium is a fifth. You can find their proportions listed under the ash portion of cat food labels.

Cats cannot form vitamin A from beta carotene, found in green and yellow vegetables, as other animals can. Save your carrots for the rabbits. Cats get vitamin A from animal products such as liver.

Don't make the harmful mistake of trying to turn your cat into a strict vegetarian. Cats are carnivores and designed to have meat in their diet. Some vital nutrients, such as taurine, are not found in vegetables.

Dietary fiber helps prevent hair balls. Try a teaspoon of canned pumpkin or a crushed graham cracker in feline milk substitute daily. Petroleum jelly works, but too much can interfere with nutrient absorption… besides, have you ever tasted it?

chapter 2

A cat is biologically designed to eat raw meat, but cooking destroys disease-producing organisms such as salmonella and toxoplasma. And who wants to eat those anyway?

Food Tip: Taurine is a valuable amino acid in a cat's diet. Supplemental doses have been shown to prevent retinal degeneration and one type of heart disease.

Fish on Fridays? Cats fed a diet exclusively of fish and fish oil can develop a rare condition called steatitis, in which the fatty layer beneath the skin becomes inflamed, making it painful to be touched. As always, a balanced diet is best.

A lamb and rice formula cat food is a good choice if your pet has a food allergy. This formula is not likely to contain fewer allergens, but a cat's exposure to this relatively new product is low, so allergic reaction is less likely.

Use common sense in feeding your cat. A nutritionally complete, balanced diet maintains a cat's proper weight and keeps your cat healthy and happy.

Is There a Cat Doctor in the House?

Cats hide pain and discomfort so well
that illness can become a guessing game.
Learn to be a good observer of
your cat's behavior.

Sherlock Holmes meets Columbo! Being a good health detective many times means getting the clues right from your cat's mouth. For instance, dry gums are an indication of dehydration. Pale, bruised, or yellow gums are signs that something isn't right. Call your vet for a checkup.

A cat's normal temperature is between 100 and 103 degrees Fahrenheit. Your vet can school you in how to take your cat's temperature. Know what is normal for your cat. Then, if the cat seems ill, you can judge if she's running a fever.

chapter 3

Cats get colds just as people do (but cats don't complain about them as much). Sneezing is one sign that your cat could have an upper respiratory infection. If the nasal discharge is thick or colored, it's time to see the vet.

Kitty Alert! Never give your cat aspirin. Acetaminophen, ibuprofen, and even children's aspirin are toxic to cats. For fever or pain symptoms, schedule a veterinary examination.

A little camouflage! If your cat treats taking medicine as an all-out war, disguise the medicine in a treat to make it more palatable. A pill can be coated with butter or mayonnaise or simply mashed into food.

A cat's normal breathing rate is twenty to thirty breaths per minute. Prolonged panting or rapid breathing are signs of respiratory distress or illness, and deserve veterinary attention.

Are there bumps on Kitty's head? If there is no other obvious cause, suspect food allergies since they often produce lesions on the head. Try a lamb and rice formula cat food for ninety days under a veterinarian's supervision.

Don't ignore sores that resist healing on your cat's ear tips or nose. These can be a sign of skin cancer, particularly in white cats. Consult a veterinarian for early treatment.

Has your cat developed an appetite for dirt? Have her checked for anemia. Dirt contains trace minerals, and your cat could be eating it for that reason.

A litter box that has become wetter than usual is a tip-off that your cat's urine production has increased. This could be a sign of kidney disease or other health problems and should be brought to the attention of your veterinarian. Symptoms of kidney disease include lethargy, weight loss, poor appetite, and an increase in thirst and urine production.

If your cat walks on the backs of her "wrists" rather than on her paws, she could have muscle weakness from a low potassium level. This is often true of cats with diabetic or kidney problems. Ask your vet about a potassium supplement.

Keep that Cheshire cat smile! Dental care is important to your cat's health. A simple rubber-toothed brush that fits over your fingertip helps remove plaque and tartar from your cat's mouth.

Open Wide! A cat's objection to having her teeth brushed is usually related to opening her mouth. Draw the lips back to expose the teeth, and brush with a circular motion. If (when) the cat struggles, stop. Try again later. Also, your veterinarian can examine and clean Kitty's teeth.

chapter 3

Gingivitis is an inflammation of the gums that is completely reversible with tooth scaling and polishing by a veterinarian. Untreated, it leads to periodontal disease, which permanently damages teeth.

Even without taxes, traffic, or troubles with the boss, cats can suffer high blood pressure. To minimize the risk, keep Kitty trim and within a proper weight range. Special low-calorie and low-sodium foods are available for the unpleasantly plump.

A magic glove! Collect a stool sample from your cat's litter box by turning a sandwich bag inside out and placing your hand inside, like you're wearing a glove. Pick up the sample, then turn the bag right side out with your other hand. Clean, quick, and bagged!

Kitty Alert! The hot line for the ASPCA National Animal Poison Control Center is (800) 548-2423. Also your veterinarian can help if you think your pet has ingested a poison.

An ounce of prevention... The bite from a black widow spider can be particularly dangerous to a cat. Prevention is preferable to treatment. Spray likely habitats with a pet-friendly pesticide, and limit your inquisitive cat's access to these places.

Keep a feline first aid kit handy for emergencies. Include round-tip scissors, gauze bandages and pads, a rectal thermometer, peroxide, and cotton balls.

Have your cat tested for feline leukemia virus (FeLV), the leading infectious cause of illness and death in cats. If the test is negative, the cat should receive a FeLV vaccination.

Fever can temporarily lighten the hair on a Siamese cat's mask—those dark areas on the face. New hair growing in a week or so after a fever is light. Normal growth and shedding bring dark hair back to the mask.

Feline leukemia virus is transmitted through saliva and contact with other cats. A positive test for the virus in one of several family cats means possible infection of the others. However, if the cats have been longtime companions, the others could be immune, especially if the others are older and have been vaccinated for FeLV in the past. Test all cats.

A whole lot of shaking going on? A cat who shakes her head constantly could have an ear mite problem. Have the cat checked by your veterinarian. Ear mites are easily treated with medication.

A cat bothered by sporadically twitching skin could be suffering from feline idiopathic epilepsy. Seizures are not usually associated with this disease, but biting the skin in the absence of fleas is. Therapy with the amino acid taurine can help.

The eyes have it! Cat eyes should look clear and bright and show a normal reaction to light. Cloudy eyes or a discharge around them are signs of problems. Eye problems call for a prompt visit to the vet.

Declawing a cat is an unnecessary and controversial procedure. It is akin to having the first finger joint cut off and leaves a cat defenseless if she gets outdoors. You can try clipping your cat's claws on a regular basis or having your veterinarian "cap" the claws with small nail covers. A groomer can also trim nails.

The best way to protect a cat's health is with an annual examination and vaccinations. Is your cat overdue for her annual checkup?

Some cats have a high-stress reaction to getting vaccinated. If this has occurred with your cat, make separate appointment times for the different vaccines so Kitty doesn't face them all at once.

Keep records of the veterinary care your cats receive. Emergencies can require after-hours help from a vet who is unfamiliar with your cat's medical history.

Alternative medical therapies such as chiropractic care and acupuncture are available for sick cats. If traditional treatments don't seem to be working, discuss other options with your veterinarian.

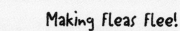

Making Fleas Flee!

More than one billion dollars are spent each year in the United States on flea-control products. Never has so much been spent on an animal so small! The tiny terrors are more than an aggravation to your cat. Because fleas feed on your cat's blood, a heavy invasion can cause anemia. While you can't "nuke 'em," you can fight back! Here's how:

❧ Flea shampoos are popular with cat owners, but if your cat resists getting bathed, try a dry, foam-type flea shampoo instead.

❧ Fleas make any cat miserable, but a cat allergic to flea bites is doubly troubled. Ask your veterinarian for a fast-acting adulticide. It impairs an adult flea's nervous system and eradicates the flea before it can bite.

❧ Some new, effective flea control products are available. Program, which is mixed into your cat's food once a month, and Advantage, which is a monthly topical applied to your cat's skin, are both available from your veterinarian. Check with your veterinarian for anything else he or she might recommend.

❧ Flea collars, shampoos, and sprays kill the adult, biting fleas. Products with an insect growth regulator, however, prevent flea eggs from hatching and break the flea's life cycle.

❧ Chemical-free Control: Natural flea collars contain extracts from plant oils and herbs. Citronella, eucalyptus, pennyroyal, and rue are some choices for making fleas rue the day.

❧ Do not use more of a shampoo, dip, or spray than the label recommends. More is not better when it comes to flea control products.

🐾 Do not combine different products, such as a flea collar and a room fogger, without consulting your veterinarian. Be chemically wise.

🐾 Unless the label states that the product is safe for both species, do not use the same flea control product on a cat and dog. Products for dogs can contain components that are harmful to cats.

🐾 With fleas, it's "So many fleas, so little time." A female has only a thirty-day life span, but can produce up to fifty eggs a day—and some eggs can lie dormant for more than six months before hatching! That's why repeated applications are necessary for effective flea control. *Semper fidelis*—be always faithful to the war on fleas!

Home Sweet Home

It's (almost) always nice
to have a cat around the house!
Here are tips on coexisting
with kitties at home.

Tiptoeing along the curtain rods, crawling under the bed, cats get into the darndest places. Choose a breakaway collar for your cat to wear so he won't get hung up or tied down during the daily adventuring.

Cats are scavengers, and one of the most enticing hunting grounds is the kitchen counter. Make sure your fearless hunter doesn't make off with a chicken bone or any such treasure that could lodge in the mouth, throat, or stomach and cause injury.

Leftovers again? Those half-used cans of cat food should be used within two or three days of opening. Bacteria multiplies quickly turning that tuna surprise into tuna yuck!

Is your house besieged and bugged by bugs at times? Remember that insecticides can cause liver damage if your cat makes a meal out of a poisoned insect. Remove dead bugs and wipe up any residual spray. Ideally, spray areas the cat won't access.

Cats always land on their feet. Right... and it never rains in California. A fall from a balcony, ledge, or railing can hurt a cat just like it hurts you. Even landing on his feet won't help if the fall is from a great height. Keep Kitty safe.

String, dental floss, and thread can be irresistible to a cat, but ingesting any of them is dangerous. String can twist or ball up in a cat's stomach or intestines and become life threatening. Pick up all loose ends around the house.

What ever happened to good ol' soap and water? Today's household cleaners can cause toxic hepatitis to any cat curious enough to sample them. Wipe up any residue from surfaces your cat could lick, and never leave cleaning solutions in pails.

A carpeted cat perch is a versatile treat for an indoor cat. Its base is a scratching and climbing post. The elevated cubbyholes provide sleeping areas, a place to play hide-and-seek, as well as a roost from which to rule the domain.

Your cat doesn't need to be a parachutist. Those drawstrings on drapes and window blinds are tempting, but can entangle a cat and cause all sorts of problems, including choking. Wrap excess cording over a high hook or bracket on the window casing out of leaping range.

A room with a view! Place your cat's perch at a window or install a sill-mounted cat seat. Cats love to survey their estates from on high, and window perches fill the bill.

It's Playtime!

Set aside time each day to play with your cat. A daily ten-minute session can even help your cat's dietary health. Picky eaters will have better appetites, and overweight cats will get needed exercise. Also, playtime relieves boredom and can control aggression. Let the games begin!

🐾 Put your playful cat in an empty bathtub with a Ping-Pong ball. The ball ricochets off the walls of the tub providing Kitty with lots of action!

🐾 Give your cat a stretchy spiral shoelace—minus the shoe—to play with. This intriguing object will tie up Kitty's attention right away! Take the lace away when Kitty shows more interest in chewing it than in playing with it.

🐾 Catnip and catnip toys are usually of interest to a cat, but lose appeal after long or frequent exposure. Offer these items to your cat only once or twice a week to keep the mystery alive.

❁ Feathers and bright ribbons are irresistible fun! Tie a feather or ribbon on a string, and tie the string to a stick or short, rounded rod. Dangle the object near the cat, or scurry it across the floor and watch what happens!

❁ Like children, cats can become overly stimulated during play. Don't end an energetic playtime abruptly. Slow the pace gradually, and your cat will be more relaxed afterward.

Does your cat keep jumping up on the kitchen counter? Make it less appealing by spreading double-sided tape on surfaces. Clearing the counter of food and small, intriguing objects also helps keep Kitty grounded. Give your cat an alternative perch near a window.

Regardless of whether they are neutered before or after puberty, 10 percent of male cats can continue to spray. If your cat sprays, don't clean up the markings with ammonia or an ammonia-based cleaner. The odor is similar to the one the cat is creating and encourages him to come back to the same spot. Use a vinegar and water solution to neutralize the odor.

Planning a Move?

Keep the cat in a separate room during the uprooting and packing to help lower stress—yours and the cat's. If professional movers are going in and out, boarding the cat—and maybe yourself—can be beneficial.

Moving is stressful for a cat. So who needs separation anxiety added in! No matter what you send ahead to a new residence, let your cat make the move with you.

Are cat box odors noticeable in the room? A dish of white vinegar neutralizes them. Place the dish on the floor in a corner of the room. Within a day you should notice the difference.

Cat hair gets everywhere, or so it seems. A damp towel or cloth removes the hair from upholstered furniture. When you brush or vacuum a fabric, do so in one direction for easier pickup.

Clean the latrine! Cat's don't like dirty bathrooms any more than you do. Clean the cat's litter box daily, and use a cat litter with little or no fragrance. Heavy scents and deodorants can repel your cat from using the litter box. Freshen it with baking soda, which is odorless.

Instead of using a cat box liner, spray the bottom and sides of the box with a nonstick cooking spray then fill with litter. This prevents the clumping-style litter from sticking to the box, making it easier to scoop!

The Six-Inch Rule: By instinct, a cat outdoors does not urinate closer than six inches to where he has defecated. So, if the perimeter of your cat's litter box seems overused, it can indicate that the cat feels crowded. Add a second litter box.

A cat who urinates on the floor or other unacceptable places may not need discipline to correct the behavior. He may need a veterinary examination. Urinating in strange places can be a sign of urinary infection, especially if the cat squats frequently and grooms himself excessively.

Cats find strong citrus scents and mentholated medicinal ointment scents offensive. Keep this in mind when you want to keep your cat away from an area or a piece of furniture. It's a harmless, natural way to mark things "off limits."

Cats and Babies

Many fears involving cats and infants are old wives' tales. Let's dispel a few and offer some tips on dealing with two-legged and four-legged little ones.

❧ First off, cats and babies can coexist safely; just use a little planning and some common sense. Make sure the cat is up to date on his vaccinations, and have him tested for parasites since some can be transmitted to humans. Make it a nonissue by having your cat checked for worms.

❧ Next, expectant mothers don't have to run and hide from the cat, fearing mysterious organisms that attack the baby she is carrying. Petting and playing and grooming are fine. The one thing an expectant mother should not do is clean the cat's litter box. That's a big no-no because there is risk of exposure to *Toxoplasma gondii*, a fancy name for an organism found in cat feces that can be harmful to a human fetus. Get Dad to clean the litter box; he'll love it.

🐾 *Toxoplasma gondii* is spread through contact with cat feces and inadvertent ingestion. In case a cat (yours or a feral cat) uses your outdoor garden as a litter box, wear rubber gloves when you garden or contact any soiled soil. Scrub garden vegetables well before cooking them.

🐾 "Old wives" also like to tell tales of insanely jealous cats plotting against babies. Feline terminators? They're not. A cat can feel displaced, just like a new father or sibling can, so be sure to show extra affection during the first few days of baby's arrival. A cat owner can ease the inevitable introduction to the new kid on the block by using baby powder and lotion long before baby comes home. Cats use their sense of smell as a means of identification. Make the baby scent "old news."

chapter 4

🐾 Finally, when was the last time you heard of a cat sucking the breath out of a baby? Even the tabloid news isn't covering that one! Common sense dictates, however, that pets and babies should be supervised when they're together. If the baby's room will be totally off-limits to the cat, start shutting off the room weeks before baby arrives home. This gives your cat a new routine to develop. And if you want to keep Kitty out of the nursery but still allow him to see and hear the baby, install a screen door.

When it comes to cats and babies, an obstetrician and veterinarian are worth consulting. Old wives telling tales in the neighborhood are not.

Let's Get Physical!

A little look at the look, physical nature,
and habits of a cat

No sweat! Cats are cool—and keep cool even though they have no sweat glands in the skin. To compensate for water loss through the kidneys, intestinal tract, and lungs, make sure your cat has plenty of fresh water.

Unlike a dog's skin, a cat's skin isn't attached to muscle. This loose-fitting "suit" helps a cat into and out of many a tight spot.

Cats are creatures of habit. A major change in the way they operate could be a signal that something is wrong. When you know your cat's hiding places, sleeping and eating patterns, and litter box procedures, you are quick to notice any deviations… unless you have an especially tricky cat!

Your cat has many ways of telling you she doesn't like her food, but shaking her head "no" while eating and flinging food from her mouth isn't one of them! If this occurs, check the cat's mouth. There could be a disease or injury to the mouth or teeth.

Ears looking at you! Cats can rotate their ears 120 degrees, and the positioning of the ears is a good mood indicator. Ears forward mean A-OK! Ears to the side indicate a perceived threat nearby. Ears back say, "I'm annoyed!" Ears pinned back indicate anger or fear—ready for attack. Ears rotating 120 degrees nonstop may indicate the cat thinks she's a bird and is trying to fly. Maybe not.

Weighty Matters: How much does your cat weigh? To find out, weigh yourself while you hold the cat. (Don't let the cat hold anything, especially not a sandwich.) Then weigh yourself alone. The difference is the cat's weight.

Do you notice pinned ears, excessive salivation, and staring into space? This could indicate that your significant other is a couch potato, but more likely—if it is in conjunction with your cat— this can indicate a stressed-out feline. A cat under stress also pants and keeps her mouth open.

Most cats don't smoke cigarettes, but many owners do. Realize that secondhand cigarette smoke contributes to feline asthma and chronic upper respiratory disease. Enforce a no smoking zone around Kitty and do both of you a favor.

Let's Get Physical

Okay, it's Bath Time!

Before you bring your cat into the bathing area, fill the sink or tub with water. The sudden sound and sight of running water can frighten a cat who has been dallying along, dirtying up, and minding her own business, so ease into it. Also, placing a rubber mat into the sink or bathtub or washtub you are using makes the cat's footing more secure.

What comes first when you bathe a longhaired cat? A battle of wills! But after that opt for a degreaser available from a professional groomer or your veterinarian. After the grease is removed, use shampoo then conditioner.

Shampoo the cat from the top of the head down to the tail and underside, being extra careful to keep soap out of the face and eyes, as you would with a baby. Any fleas will flee the water, so starting at the cat's head drives the pests down the cat into the sink instead of up into the cat's face and ears. Use the sink hose or a hand-held wand designed for dishes or showering to make rinsing the cat fast and easy. Towel dry, then blow dry on a gentle setting and Kitty is ready for a big night out on the town!

Your cat's coat is a good indicator of how things are running beneath it. A scruffy appearance, bald patches, or redness of the skin can mean illness, parasites, or allergies.

Cats are not interested in diet fads nor in getting thin enough to walk down a Paris fashion runway. Yet, cats can suffer from anorexia. In this case, the term means loss of appetite. An anorexic cat might be ill, but stress can cause feline anorexia, too.

Very heady material. Cats have one of two head shapes (unless you have a two-headed cat): round or triangular. Look at your cat's head. The first head type is very circular when viewed from the front. The second can vary in degree but is wedge-shaped.

The Scratching Syndrome: Cats need to scratch and flex their claws, but they don't have to exercise on the family upholstery. Nubby, textured fabrics are most appealing, while flat, tightly woven cottons are less likely to be attractive. Commercial or homemade scratching posts, vertical wooden objects, or carpet-covered boxes and posts make happy alternatives to the family couch. Another favorite? Thick strips of corrugated cardboard!

Is Kitty licking the water faucet instead of using the water dish? Cats exhibiting this behavior could have a depth perception problem when drinking clear water from a bowl. Try using a patterned water dish or a drop of food coloring in the water.

Cleanliness Is Next to Kittiness

Normally, a cat is a self-cleaning machine who can take care of her own grooming needs. Exceptions are longhaired cats, ill or obese cats, or cats with fleas or hair balls. There is nothing quite so inelegant as a hair ball, so here's a quick guide to keeping your cat clean, coiffured, and cultured!

🐾 To keep the fur of a smooth-coated cat, such as a Siamese, in good condition, use a chamois cloth.

🐾 If your cat has prominent eyes, like a Persian's, it's a good idea to wipe her face gently with a damp washcloth each day.

🐾 Clumping litters can make messy situations for longhaired cats. Trim the south end of your northbound Persian to make grooming easier.

❧ Brushing matted hair out of a cat's coat is possible, but use a wide-toothed comb or a groomer's rake, which has long, blunt teeth.

❧ The Coat and Glove Treatment: Grooming gloves are an innovation in the area of cat-grooming products. The gloves gently remove loose hair and give your cat the sensation of being petted as you groom.

❀ Most longhaired cats benefit from daily grooming to keep the coat healthy and free of loose hairs. Left ungroomed, longhaired coats mat easily, and removing mats is a difficult, painful, process. Regular brushing works better. A few longhaired breeds, such as the Balinese, Somali, and ragdoll, can be groomed once or twice a week—nature makes them generally mat-resistant! Longhaired white cats need daily grooming to stay as clean as the driven snow—it's easier to prevent stains and marks than to remove them! Also, monthly bathing for any longhair is a good schedule to maintain.

♣ To safely trim your cat's nails, use a nail clipper designed for cats. Do not use household scissors or family nail clippers. Press gently on the foot pads to extend the nail out. Clip only the clear part. Nicking the pink quick is very painful and causes bleeding.

Grooming can be a pleasurable interaction between you and your cat. Holding and petting should be the first part of the process as it makes everything that follows easier. Start with a ten-minute session the first day and work up to a longer pampering. Cats think it's neat to be neat!

The Kitten Korner

The pouncing, bubbly, tumbling, twisty,
wild, and winsome world of kittens

Bringing home a new kitten? Provide the necessary equipment as you would provide a layette for a baby. A cat carrier, a litter box with low sides, a comfy bed with washable bedding, and an adjustable collar with an ID tag are good starter items. You can forgo the talcum powder and diapers.

The Kitten Korner

The first milk produced by a mother cat is critical for her newborn kittens. If nursing problems appear, try to hold off feeding the kittens a replacement formula until after the first few days of life.

A nursing bottle for pets is the best way to feed a newborn kitten who cannot nurse from his mother. Using a medicine dropper can cause replacement formula to enter the kitten's lungs, which can lead to pneumonia. If the kitten's sucking reflexes are too weak to allow sucking from a bottle feeder, ask a veterinarian how to use an infant feeding tube.

Kittens are wildly curious and rambunctious. Before allowing your new fluff ball to have run of the house, look high and low for potential dangers. Plop down on the floor to spot low-lying hazards such as electrical cords or to see tight spaces under appliances that could entrap tiny paws. Look up high for hazards on the mantel, bookcase, or atop the refrigerator. Kittens are ingenious when it comes to mischief!

Roughhousing with your kitten only encourages aggressive adult behavior later on. If a kitten learns that hands and feet are things to pounce upon or defend against, you might be facing ankle ambushes and nips long after you have forgotten the "game."

The Kitten Korner

Scratching is a normal, necessary behavior, but no one likes drapes or furniture in tatters. Give your kitten early experiences with appropriate surfaces, such as carpeted mats, corrugated cardboard pads, and carpeted posts. These can prevent your kitten from discovering the joys of upholstered furniture.

Tots need shots, and kittens do, too! Plan your first visit to the vet as Kitty reaches eight to nine weeks of age. Upper respiratory viruses and distemper can be prevented with a series of three vaccinations by the age of sixteen weeks.

chapter 6

Kittens make lousy satchels, and their legs make terrible handles. Never pick up a kitten by the scruff of his neck or by his legs. Gentle handling lets a kitten know there's nothing to fear and grows a cat who is gentle and affectionate.

Kittens love to climb. Tie shut the legs of a pair of old blue jeans and stuff the jeans to the waist with old rags. Hang them on the back of a chair and it's Kitty Everest time!

Kittens come with a built in "Litter Box Alert." Show your new family member the litter box and he knows how to use it, naturally. If your kitten is tiny, cut a low entry on the pan's side or buy one with low sides so he won't get discouraged trying to get inside.

A kitten orphaned under the age of six weeks needs a surrogate mother for nursing. If you find an orphan, call your veterinarian. For immediate fostering, you can bottle-feed the orphan with a premixed kitten formula available from pet stores. Avoid feeding cow's milk to a kitten. It won't cause mooing, but it does cause diarrhea!

Bottle-feeding a kitten might require some patience (squirming and spitting aside). Hold the kitten at a 45-degree angle on his tummy and stimulate his mouth with the bottle nipple until the kitten takes it and begins sucking. Bubbles form around the mouth when a kitten is full. Don't lay a kitten on his back to nurse. This causes choking.

You can begin weaning an orphaned kitten from the bottle at four weeks of age. Pour formula into a dish and let the kitten become accustomed to lapping it. Gradually, add canned food to the dish formula.

Kittens go through a socialization period during the first eight weeks of life. If there are other cats in the household, introduce the new kitten to them during this time.

Like everything else in life, weaning doesn't happen all at once. A five-week-old toddling ball of fur can eat solid food three times a day and still want to nurse or drink from a bottle. You can gradually replace canned food with nutritious dry food and grow a full-sized cat.

Unless you are serious about breeding cats, spaying or neutering is the best course of action for your kitten's well-being. The procedure can be done early, at the time of the second round of vaccinations, about twelve weeks of age. Talk to your vet about a sensible schedule.

Most adult cats tolerate a bouncing, bubbly, rolling fluff ball in the household more readily than they would a new adult cat. Kittens don't threaten the established hierarchy like grown cats do.

chapter 6

An upper respiratory infection is extremely contagious. Do not put a kitten in contact with an adult cat, particularly one recovered from a recent respiratory problem, because that cat is a carrier. Protect your kitten by isolating him when he is too young for immunization.

The world can be a very scary place to an orphaned kitten. If you are caring for an orphan, give him a small fuzzy toy to sleep with. This simulates the missing littermates and helps the kitten adapt to his new world.

Trying to find homes for a mother's latest litter? Carefully screen all potential new owners. Make sure the kittens are placed with responsible and loving people. A kitten is a new family member, not a toy or cute novelty for the moment.

Kittens are imaginative in their play and don't need expensive toys. A crumpled ball of paper or an empty paper bag placed on its side are irresistible adventures! And have you ever watched a kitten bat a plastic straw or ballpoint pen barrel across a kitchen floor? Get ready to jump out of the way!

Kittens are made out of love. Treat them accordingly!

The Not-so-Great Outdoors

The great outdoors is not-so-great for cats. Outdoor living exposes your cat to fights, diseases, and people with autos. Here are some things to keep in mind if your cat is roaming the outdoors.

If your cat spends time outdoors and has free access to your garden and lawn, use pesticides and fertilizers responsibly. Never spray or spread chemicals when the cat is nearby, and consider organic options whenever possible. Cats and garden chemicals don't mix!

chapter 7

Uninvited House Guests: Fleas hitch a ride on your outdoor cat and pay you a visit indoors. To stop the open door policy, consider using a nontoxic yard spray or a beneficial nematode spray from the pet store. Beneficial nematodes are natural predators of preadult fleas. You don't have to spray the entire lawn, but concentrate on the areas where your cat spends most of her time. Pay special attention to shady areas; fleas don't like sunlight.

Cats don't have green thumbs when it comes to gardening, but many think they do and take to "improving" your garden by digging in it. If you have a different vision, make Kitty her own sandbox on the garden perimeter as a distraction, or plant some marigolds and chamomile in the garden. They give off a scent cats dislike.

Travel Tips

Whether it's a weekend trip, a household move, or a short trip to the vet, you will, at some time, travel with your cat. Here are some things to remember for outdoor excursions.

❀ If a car ride turns your docile tabby into a raging tiger, try dosing the interior of the cat carrier with catnip.

❀ Feed your cat several hours before you take a long car trip. A meal just before departing increases the chance of an upset stomach. You can feed light meals along the way.

❀ Take a pause that refreshes! If an upcoming trip means that your cat is confined in a cat carrier for many hours, take periodic breaks and let your cat stretch her legs and move about. Keep her safely harnessed and leashed even inside the car.

🐾 Safety Tip: Strap your cat's carrier to the seat, or keep your cat safe in a cat seat belt—the safest models feature a harness, not a collar, attached to an anchoring strap. In an auto collision or abrupt stop, an unanchored cat carrier can be hurled throughout the car—with your cat inside.

🐾 On a do-it-yourself move, don't transport your cat in the cargo area of a van. Kitty needs to be in a carrier in the passenger cab or in a car that follows.

🐾 Because the taste and smell of water varies from place to place, fill a large jug with your cat's usual tap water before moving to a new location. A cat often refuses to drink unfamiliar water.

🐾 Train kittens to travel! Introduce your kitten to brief car rides. Use a cat carrier and allow the kitten to become acquainted with the new sights, sounds, and smells. Later, you will have a more relaxed adult traveler.

Keep a lid on it—the garbage, that is! Cats are not strict gourmets and chew on food-encrusted string, plastic, or foil wrap. If swallowed, these materials can cause life-threatening intestinal blockages. Wrap the trash and put it in a closed garbage can so your outdoor adventurer doesn't get into trouble.

For outdoor cats or those in multicat households, it is recommended to vaccinate against FIP—Feline Infectious Peritonitis. Once contracted, there is no cure. The preventive vaccine is given as nose drops.

Wouldn't you know it; cats are attracted to the motion of snakes! If you suspect a snake bite, your pet has the best chance at recovery if you get her to the vet *immediately*. Don't lose precious time by attempting first aid yourself.

The Kitty Crop: If your outdoor cat likes catnip, grow her own patch in the garden! Other good choices are cat thyme and garden heliotrope. Cats are attracted to these fragrances.

Unless your cat lives strictly indoors, there is a risk she could be exposed to rabies, a fatal virus. If your cat has access to the outdoors, vaccinate against rabies.

Keep your garden beds moist with mulch if you want to discourage your outdoor cat from digging. Cats don't "dig" damp substances.

Outdoor cats can contract Lyme disease from certain ticks that are infected. If you live in a high incidence area, prevent exposure with a daily tick check. The bacteria is not transmitted from the tick until it has been attached to your cat for ten to twelve hours.

Feline immunodeficiency virus—feline AIDS—is spread through bite wounds during cat fights. A vaccine has not yet been developed to prevent the disease. Avoiding exposure to infected cats is the only protection, something more easily accomplished if the cat is kept indoors.

The Lost and Found

An outdoor cat can become a wanderer and get wrapped up in new discoveries. Usually, however, the cat's intelligence and territorial instinct guides her back home. Yet, untold thousands of cats become lost and adopt a different territory, wander into new homes, or are turned in to shelters. Here are some tips to have your lost (or otherwise occupied) cat returned to you.

🐾 Only a small percentage of cats turned in to shelters are returned to their owners. An identification tag is your cat's—and your—best friend. Improve your cat's chances of being returned by using a breakaway collar and a visible ID tag.

WARNING: Tattooed Cat

❧ If your cat objects to a hanging ID tag, look for an alternative. Some attach to the collar's surface and some collars can be embroidered with your cat's name, rank, and serial number.

❧ Consider purchasing an ID tag that includes a toll-free registry service. If your cat is lost, the finder can call the number and you will be contacted by the service.

❧ A microchip implanted beneath the skin is a permanent means of identification that does not require a collar. The chip stores medical and identifying information on a biomedical capsule no bigger than a grain of rice. The information is retrieved with a compatible scanner. Back up any implanted microchip ID with a traditional pet tag that lists the microchip number and the toll-free database hot line.

🐾 An unfortunate fact of life is that cats are stolen and sold to researchers. A tattooed cat, being registered and easy to identify is less appealing to a catnapper. Tattoo-A-Pet is a nationwide protection service that performs the painless procedure, usually on the cat's ear, belly, or the inside part of a leg. They maintain registry and can be reached at (800) 828-8667.

🐾 Make a cat identity card for your pet. Take several photos from all angles. Write a complete description of the cat, including head shape, body type, color and markings, weight, age, and sex. This can be invaluable in helping you locate a lost cat.

ORANGE TABBY • HANDSOME MALE • AGE 3

BUTCH

Special Considerations

From litter-ary matters,
to managing a multicat household,
to keeping a cat happy during holidays,
here are some splendid ideas for dealing
with your very special cat.

It is a special circumstance when a cat stops using his litter box and begins treating other areas as a bathroom. If this occurs, first rule out illness. If all is well, make sure the litter box is tidy; a cat needs things neat and clean. If the behavior persists, there is something the cat doesn't like. Experiment with different litter box sizes, types of litter filler, and new locations for the box.

A trail of footprints? If your cat tracks litter away from the litter box, place the box on an artificial turf doormat. The blades of "grass" catch the litter as the cat walks away.

If you like using a liner in your cat's litter box, but the cat's claws slit the liner into useless shreds, line the liner with folded newspaper sections.

Special Considerations

For an older cat with mobility problems, getting into a litter box can be difficult. An entry ramp leading into the box is a big help. Be sure to keep the litter level high so your cat can make an easy exit as well.

Cats don't fast. Just because a cat is fat doesn't mean he can go without eating. An obese cat who stops eating runs the risk of developing hepatic lipidosis—a fatty liver disease. A halt in the eating routine calls for a visit to the vet.

Is your cat door being used by some uninvited guests such as raccoons or skunks? Keep a night-light burning. Wild critters are usually discouraged by well-lit rooms.

If your cat goes on a hunger strike when left in the care of someone else, precondition him to eat at the sound of a bell. In the beginning, start to ring a bell before each meal, so Kitty associates the sound with the feeding. The sound of the bell becomes more important than the person who rings it.

Here a Cat, There a Cat!

One cat is a companion, two are a family, and three or more are tumbling, toddling bundles of fur and fun... and a few squabbles! If there is more than one cat in the household, here are some things to keep in mind:

❦ Instinct tells a cat to find a place within the social order so his right to food and shelter is not constantly challenged. There can be a little squabbling while the order is being established.

❦ Cats in a multicat household show aggression if they have no other way to jockey for position. Try using multilevel perches and towers so your dominant cats can physically "rule the roost." The top cat takes the highest perch.

❧ Acknowledge your top cat's role, and he will spend less time asserting himself over the other cats. Feed the dominant cat first; pet him first. Lavish extra attention on the others when the boss is away.

❧ When it comes to establishing a pecking order, a male and a female cat have the least to argue about. Two unrelated males have the greatest chance of fighting when first introduced.

❧ One litter box per cat, plus an extra box, is the best formula for a multicat household. This minimizes accidents and discourages behavioral problems from developing.

❧ Prepare a separate room for a newly arriving cat. Give him time to feel secure in his own space before opening the door to the rest of the house and the new companions.

❧ If friendships and understandings are slow to form between a newcomer and the established cats, feed the cats in separate areas. If they have less anxiety about eating, they may feel less threatened at other times.

❋ Before introducing a new cat to your other cats, try this "getting to know you" procedure. Rub each cat with a separate cloth to pick up each cat's particular scent. Place the old timers' cloths in a separate room with the new cat, and give the resident cats the cloth scented by the newcomer. This lessens the surprise of a new face.

Special considerations

Introduce your cat to a new residence the same way you would bring a new cat into your old home. Confine your cat to one room at first then allow him to prowl the rest of the residence on his own time frame. Shortly, the cat takes over again!

Your move to a new area can mean getting new medical care for your pets. Remember to travel with your cat's veterinary records so your new vet does not have to wait for your previous vet to mail them.

chapter 8

Consider thoroughly cleaning the carpeting in a new residence before moving in. Urine odors embedded deep in the carpeting from previous cats can attract your cat to the same spots. Don't give bad habits a chance to start.

For your cat's well-being, and to save wear and tear on the furniture, your cat should have a scratching pad or post. To make an inexpensive homemade version, you need only three materials: a piece of plywood or pressed wood board, a stapler, and some canvas such as that used to make latch-hook rugs. Simply staple several layers of rug canvas on the board and listen for the sound of claws scratching!

For Happy Holidays!

Holidays and special occasion days mean a big change in your pet's routine. These common sense considerations can keep your four-footed friends happy, too!

🐾 Halloween costumes are tricky and offer no treat for a cat. Spare your cat the stress of dressing up.

🐾 If fireworks are part of your Fourth of July or Cinco de Mayo celebrations, bring your outdoor cats inside beforehand. Pyrotechnics are dangerous and frightening to animals.

❧ Parties and celebrations? Cats crave quiet sophistication. If your parties run more to the raucous and rambunctious, do your feline family member a favor and put Kitty in a separate room with food, water, and a litter box. Unusual household noisemaking can be frightening.

Special Considerations

❧ If roast turkey is part of the day's menu, make sure anything the cat gobbles is free of bones. Never let your cat snack directly off turkey bones; they are soft, can splinter, and cause choking. After your feast, dispose of the remains in a lidded (cat-proof) trash can before you reach for the Alka-Seltzer.

❧ The lower branches of a Christmas tree are a cat's hunting ground. Hang your soft ornaments on these branches, since delicate ornaments don't last long around cats. Hanging strips of lemon or orange peel can repel a cat's advances. The citrus smell is unappealing to cats.

❖ A Christmas tree is a feline amusement park, jungle safari, mountain climb, and shooting gallery all at once! Anchor the tree top with a ceiling hook to avoid sounds of "Timbe-r-r-r!" during the holidays.

Special considerations

❧ Your household Santa Claws creates a lively playground out of the wrapping paper strewn around the living room on Christmas morning. Be sure to clear out ribbons and bows that can twist around a cat's neck or limbs.

❧ Kitty Alert! Angel hair and tinsel are hazardous materials to curious cats. Holly is poisonous, and the berries are bad news, too. It's best not to use them in decorating.

❧ If a new cat or kitten is on Santa's list, arrange for a gift certificate to come down the chimney. Redeem it after the holidays when the household is back to normal and not so overwhelming to a cat.

Make your holidays joyful for everyone in the house!

Babies and toddlers should learn by example how to pet a cat. Rough handling or teasing forces a cat to defend himself. Little ones need to know the difference between a soft toy and a live cat.

And remember... Old blankets and towels make good bedding for a cat. Clean out your linen closet and send any extras to your local animal shelter or rescue organization to make a homeless cat's life a little better.

For more fun facts and authoritative advice about cats, including health-care advice, grooming tips, training advice, and insights into the special joys and overcoming the unique problems of cat ownership, go to your local pet shop, bookstore, or newsstand and pick up your copy of *Cat Fancy* magazine today.

BowTie™ Press is a division of Fancy Publications, which is the world's largest publisher of pet magazines. For further information on your favorite pets, look for *Cats USA, Kittens USA, Dog Fancy, Dogs USA, Puppies USA, Bird Talk, Horse Illustrated, Reptiles, Aquarium Fish, Rabbits, Ferrets USA,* and many more.